WORKBOOK
FOR

ATOMIC
HABITS

AN EASY & PROVEN WAY TO BUILD GOOD HABITS & BREAK BAD ONES

By
JAMES CLEAR

JESSICA BRIDGE

Table of Contents

HOW TO USE THIS WORKBOOK

This workbook has an important goal of helping you understand that you can control, change and define your habits. This workbook significantly opens your eyes to see the endless possibilities that exist in self-development, attitude formation and habit building.

However, you only get to enjoy this when you sincerely respond to the questions from each chapter. Not only will these questions give you reasons to reflect and decide to take your habits in your hands, responding to them will help you realize that you are actually in control, thereby making you become intentional with your habits.

Each chapter is introduced with essential points. With this, the most striking points are made available at your fingertips. So, relax and enjoy your workbook. By diligently carrying out the exercises given to you, you are guaranteed a lifetime of healthy, regulated habits.

INTRODUCTION

Atomic habits is a book that will help you live a better life by taking charge of your habits and all that your habits determine. You will enjoy clarity, direction and a sense of purpose as you go through the pages of this amazing book.

The principles outlined in this book have been tested and trusted to help you take charge of your life through your very own habits. You'll learn to improve the good habits and eliminate those that are of no good to you.

This book is divided into four broad sections, each consisting of a law with five chapters each. Each section adequately handles all that you need to know about successful behavior change, how to achieve it and much more.

Who should read this?

If you desire to sit in the pilot seat of your life, able to control your actions and not unnecessarily blown about by every wind of habit, this book is for you.

No one knows it all. With Atomic Habits however, you can know a whole lot about your life, time, decisions and attitudes that you hitherto did not pay attention to.

What's in it for me and why is it important?

If you go through with reading and practicing all that this book has to offer, you'll discover that your life becomes easier. And better.

You will soon discover:

- You're not the only one who needs help
- You can become a better person
- You can control your behavior by applying simple steps
- Change is possible
- Time is powerful
- Your identity is tied to your behavior
- Doing the right thing is easy
- The systems in your life matter

Chapter One: The Surprising Power of Atomic Habits

Here are some key points we learned in this chapter:

- Your fate can change once you set out to do things aright. Precept upon precept, line by line, your story can turn around.

- If you're willing to become a better person, begin by building upon your little improvements. If you are able to break down all the energies that go into whatever project you've decided to embark on, and you're also able to improve it by a single percent; when you put them together, you will get a huge increase.

- You can become a much better person by making tiny adjustments to the areas of your life that are often overlooked. In addition, the results you've desired for quite some time would come faster than you've imagined.

- If you repeat little errors, continue to make poor decisions and duplicate tiny mistakes every day, the only thing your choices will produce in the long run are toxic results. Accumulating many correct steps results in a breakthrough. Sadly, accumulating many missteps only births problems.

- By making simple changes to your daily habits, your life can be transformed and transported to a whole, different destination.

- Currently, the extent to which you are successful or otherwise holds no water. However, what is important is whether your current habits are thrusting you towards success, or not.

- To predict where you'll end up in life, do just one thing- follow the curve of tiny gains or tiny losses. Then watch and see how your seemingly insignificant choices will accumulate several years down the line.
- The gap between failure and success is magnified by time. Time multiplies whatever it's fed.
- You make time your friend when you breed great habits. The reverse becomes the case when you breed bad habits.
- Breakthroughs do not occur randomly. Several past actions which were in charge of building up the potential required to unleash a major change cause a breakthrough.
- For your habits to make differences which would be considered meaningful, you must be persistent enough to break through the Plateau of Latent potential.

Answer the following questions as sincerely as you can:

1. One week from now, what systems are you willing to follow in order to achieve success? Will you lead healthy eating habits that affect your weight positively? Will you practice little financial habits that will positively affect your financial life in the long run? What will you do? Write them down.

_____

_____

_____

_____

_____

_____

2. Systems are important, but goals are more important. **True [ ] False [ ]**

3. Your outcomes are a lagging measure of one of the following. **Goals [ ] Systems [ ] Habits [ ]**

4. Do you believe that you can achieve success by making little adjustments in the areas of your life where you need help? **Yes [ ] No [ ]**

5. If your response to question '4' above was 'Yes', state the areas of your life to which you are willing to make these adjustments.

   _____

   _____

   _____

   _____

   _____

6. If your response to question '4' above was 'No', state the reasons for which you believe that making little adjustments in the areas of your life where you need help will do little to help you achieve success.

   _____

   _____

_____

_____

_____

_____

7. Have you been dismissing small changes in your life
   because they do not seem to bring about any
   improvements? **Yes [ ]   No [ ]**

8. In what areas of your life have you been dismissing the
   changes addressed by question 7 above?

_____

_____

_____

_____

_____

9. What bad habits have you struggled to change for so long?
   State them here.

_____

_____

_____

_____

_____

10. Going forward, how do you plan to focus on your systems
    rather than on setting goals?

Chapter Two: How Your Habits Shape Your Identity (and Vice Versa)

Here are some key points we learned in this chapter:

- We often face challenges in the process of changing habits because we try to change the wrong thing, or focus on changing our habits the wrong way.

- By focusing on building habits based on identity, you commence the process of changing habits.

- Every system of actions is backed by a system of beliefs.

- No behavior will last if it remains different from your self.

- You must change the underlying beliefs that resulted in your past behavior if you wat to change your habits, if not, changing your habits would be very difficult.

- A successful change of your behavior begins by changing who you are.

- The highest form of intrinsic motivation is attained when your habits are now a part of your identity.

- It is one thing to say you are a type of person who wants a particular identity. It is another to say you are the type of person who is, and who carries a particular identity. Know this!

- The greater the pride you have in a particular aspect of your identity, the greater your motivation will be to uphold the habits related to it.

- The true change of behavior is identity change.

- Identity sustains habits started by motivation.

- Until improvements become a part of you, they are temporary.
- What you do is an indication of the type of person you believe you are.
- It is easy to do the right thing.
- The depth with which a thought or action is tied to your identity defines the extent of its difficulty to be changed.
- Your self-image getting in the way is the actual reason why you fail to stick with habits.
- Out of your habits emerges your identity.
- Continuous repetition of any behavior emphasizes the identity connected to that behavior.
- The more evidence you have for a belief, the more strongly you will believe it.

Answer the following questions as sincerely as you can:

1. Having understood that your habits shape your identity, what are you willing to restructure about yourself? Will you continue to make statements that suggest that your identity is different from your goal? Will you decide to no longer identify as your former person? What changes are you willing to make? Pen them down.

_____

_____

_____

_____

_____

_____

2. Changing your outcomes before changing your identity will help you change your habits successfully. **True [ ]   False [ ]**

3. The correct order to achieving lasting behavioral change is:
   a. **Outcome- Identity- Processes**
   b. **Identity- Processes- Outcomes**
   c. **Processes- Outcomes- Identity**

4. Based on what you have learnt about identity, what kind of person are you?

   _____

   _____

   _____

   _____

   _____

   _____

5. What norms have been attached to your identity all your life?

   _____

   _____

   _____

   _____

   _____

   _____

6. What practical steps do you intend to implement in order to redefine those norms?

_____

_____

_____

_____

_____

_____

7. Fill the blank spaces below with your desired achievements of who you are each time you do something worthwhile.

Each time I _____, I am a_____

Each time I _____, I am a_____

Each time I _____, I am a_____

8. What do you want to stand for?

_____

_____

_____

_____

_____

_____

9. Who do you wish to become?

_____

_____

_____

_____

_____

_____

10. What identity do you want to reinforce today with the habits you've chosen? State it!

_____

_____

_____

_____

_____

_____

Chapter Three: How to Build Better Habits in 4 Simple Steps

Here are some key points we learned in this chapter:

- A behavior which has been repeated time and again that it has become automatic is defined as a habit.
- Trial and error begin the process of habit formation.
- When repeatedly faced with a problem, inevitably, your brain begins to automate the process of solving such problem.
- Habits are series of automatic solutions which solve problems and stresses that you face on a regular basis.
- Habits have an ultimate purpose- solving the problems of life with the littlest energy and effort.
- Any habit at all can be broken down into a feedback loop consisting of these four steps: cue, craving, response, and reward.
- A simple set of rules that can be employed to build better habits are the four laws of behavior change.
- As habits are created, the level of activity in the brain decreases.
- A habit is simply a memory of the steps you followed in the past to solve a problem.
- In order to predict what will work in the future, the brain remembers the past.
- Building habits and attaining freedom are corresponding.
- Habits do not restrict freedom. They create freedom.

- In order for your behavior to become a habit, it must be sufficient at each stage.
- The systems present in your life shape your habit.
- Every habit serves the purpose of solving the problems you face.
- The four stages of cue, craving, response, and reward influence nearly everything we do each day.
- For every moment you remain alive, the four-step process is running and active.
- Your mind looks out for rewards as it repeatedly analyzes your internal and external environment searching for clues of where rewards are located.
- People are different, and as such are not motivated by the same set of cues.

Answer the following questions as sincerely as you can:

1. Forming a habit will involve series of trial and error processes. Your brain will also have to make decisions for you whenever you encounter a new situation in life. How do you intend to go about solving problems that you are not sure of? Will you shy away from such? Will you try things to see what works out? Pen them down.

_____

_____

_____

_____

_____

_____

2. Your brain is always working to preserve your conscious attention for whatever task is least essential. **True [ ]   False [ ]**

3. The stages through which habits proceed are:

   a. **Response- Craving- Cue- Reward**

   b. **Reward- Cue- Craving- Response**

   c. **Cue- Craving- Response- Reward**

   d. **Craving- Cue- Response- Reward**

4. What cues have you been paying attention to lately? Write them down.

   _____

   _____

   _____

   _____

   _____

   _____

5. Consider your cravings. What change in state would you say they deliver? Write them down in this order.

Cravings	**Change in state**
1. _____	_____
2. _____	_____
3. _____	_____

6. Can you identify those elements that trigger your cravings?
   Yes [ ]   No [ ]

7. If your response to question 7 above was **yes**, list the elements that trigger your cravings below.

   _____

   _____

   _____

   _____

   _____

   _____

8. If your response to question 7 above was **no**, are you willing to discover the elements that trigger your cravings? **Yes [ ] No [ ]**

9. What habits are you interested in developing? State them here.

   _____

   _____

   _____

   _____

   _____

   _____

10. Do you think you are capable of building the habits listed in question 9 above?

Yes [ ]   No [ ]

11. Give reasons for your choice in question 10.

_____

_____

_____

_____

_____

_____

Chapter Four: The Man Who Didn't Look Right

Here are some key points we learned in this chapter:

- The human brain takes in all of your surroundings continuously, analyzing every bit of information it comes across.

- Anytime you experience something continuously, your brain starts to notice the important details which it catalogs for future use.

- By practicing enough, you can pick up on the cues that envisage certain outcomes without intentionally thinking about it.

- There is more to you than your conscious self.

- A habit can begin even without you being aware of the cue.

- You are capable of taking note of an opportunity and taking action without paying conscious attention to it.

- As habits begin to form, your actions come under the course of both your automatic and your nonconscious mind.

- Over time, the prompts that trigger our habits become so common that they are basically invisible.

- To arrive at a point where we can effectively build new habits, we must get a grip on our existing habits.

- You cannot expect to improve a habit that remains mindless.

- When a behavior becomes more and more automatic, the likelihood that you are going to consciously think about it becomes slimmer.

- Lack of self- awareness can be blamed for many of our failures in performance.
- In other to change bad habits, the first step to take is being on the lookout for them.
- Speaking your bad habits out loud makes the consequences appear more real.
- By engaging the Pointing-and-Calling technique, you raise your level of awareness from a nonconscious habit to a more conscious level.
- The Habits Scorecard is a simple exercise you can use to become more aware of your behavior.

Answer the following questions as sincerely as you can:

1. The human brain is powerful enough to pick up cues that predict certain outcomes without you necessarily thinking about it in the moment. What are the seemingly unconscious activities that go on in your life that you're willing to make conscious note of? Chewing your nails? Picking your nose? Completing people's sentences? Whatever they are, state them here.

_____

_____

_____

_____

_____

_____

2. What does the process of behavior change begin with?
   a. Awareness
   b. Habits
   c. Action
   d. Cues

3. Hunger and appetite are consciously governed. **True [   ] False [ ]**

4. Are you willing to get a handle on your current habits in order to effectively build new ones? **Yes [ ]   No [ ]**

5. If your response to question 4 above was *yes*, how do you intend to go about achieving this?

   _____

   _____

   _____

   _____

   _____

   _____

6. If your response to question 4 above was *no*, why do you believe it is impossible for you to get a handle on your current habits?

   _____

   _____

   _____

   _____

_____

_____

7. What do you think about pointing- and- calling? Is this a
   strategy you're willing to adopt, going forward?

   _____

   _____

   _____

   _____

   _____

   _____

8. What are your daily habits? List them below.

   a. _____

   b. _____

   c. _____

   d. _____

   e. _____

   f. _____

   g. _____

   h. _____

   i. _____

   j. _____

9. Based on the list created in question 8 above, examine whether each habit is good, bad or neutral by placing the following signs in front of each list: '+' if it is a good habit, '-' if it is a bad habit, and '=' if it is a neutral habit. E.g., *Take a nap* =

a. _____

b. _____

c. _____

d. _____

e. _____

f. _____

g. _____

h. _____

i. _____

j. _____

10. What bad habits do you want to change by looking out for them? List them below.

_____

_____

_____

_____

_____

_____

Chapter Five: The Best Way to Start a New Habit

Here are some key points we learned in this chapter:

- Implementation intention is a plot made ahead of time about when and where to act.

- Implementation intentions are efficient in ensuring that we stick to our goals.

- There is a greater likelihood that those who make a precise plan for when and where they will perform a new habit would go through, as opposed to those who do not.

- By choosing to be specific about what you want and how you will achieve them, you learn how to say no to the things that will slow your progress down, cause distractions and take you off your course.

- When your dreams are vague, you find it easy to rationalize little exceptions all day long. You will hardly even get around to the exact things you need to do to succeed.

- One of the most practical ways to build a new habit is to identify habits you do each day, and then stack your new behavior on top of them.

- Practicing habit stacking allows you to create a chain of simple rules that guide your future behavior.

- The major secret to successfully creating a habit stack is choosing the right cue to kick things.

- A practical way to identify the right trigger for your habit stack is coming up with a list of your current habits.

- Habit stacking works best when the cue is highly specific and immediately actionable.
- Habit stacking intensifies the chances that you'll most likely stick with a habit, by stacking your new behavior on top of an old one.
- If your new habit is well and tightly bound to a specific cue, the odds that you will notice when the time comes to act are higher.
- Implementation intentions and habit stacking strategies are among the best hands-on ways to create noticeable cues for your habits and design a clear plan for when and where to take action.
- No behavior ever occurs isolated of the other. Each action becomes a cue that triggers the next behavior.

Answer the following questions as sincerely as you can:

1. Over the next few days, what specific plans will you make for where and when you will perform a new habit? Are you going to lean on your motivation, or will you simply remember to do them? Whatever it is, state it here.

_____

_____

_____

_____

_____

_____

2. It is always obvious when and where to take action. **True [ ]
False [ ]**

3. Most people think they lack motivation. In the true sense of things however, what they lack is: **Clarity [ ]   Implementation [ ]   Intention [ ]   Meditation [ ]**

4. List five habits you will apply the implementation intention strategy to over the next seven days.

a. _____

b. _____

c. _____

d. _____

e. _____

5. List five implementation intentions you're willing to set during the next seven days using this format: *When I have my bath, I will comb my hair.*

a. _____

b. _____

c. _____

d. _____

e. _____

6. Identify five habits you do every day.

a. _____

b. _____

c. _____

d. _____

e. _____

7. Create a habit stack for each of the habits listed in question 6 above. E.g; _Marriage. After I get into bed at night, I will give my partner a kiss._

    a. _____
    b. _____
    c. _____
    d. _____
    e. _____

8. What new behaviors will you include in the middle of the routine created in question 7? State them here.

    a. _____
    b. _____
    c. _____
    d. _____
    e. _____

Chapter Six: Motivation is Overrated, Environment Often Matters More

Here are some key points we learned in this chapter:

- Your habits are subject to change on the basis of the room you are in, and the cues before you.

- An invisible hand capable of shaping human behavior is the environment.

- Regardless of what our unique personalities are, there are certain behaviors which tend to arise over and over again under certain environmental conditions.

- The greatest form of change is not internal, but external. The world around us changes us.

- You are more likely to try a product or service based on how obviously available it is.

- We love to believe we call the shots and are in control. Funny enough, most of the actions we take on a daily basis are shaped by the most obvious option, and not by purposeful drive and choice.

- Every living being is blessed with its own methods of sensing and understanding the world. Of all the sensory abilities however, the most powerful is vision.

- A small change in what you see can lead to a big shift in what you do.

- It becomes easy to ignore a habit with hidden, or subtle cues.

- When you sprinkle triggers throughout your surroundings, the odds that you'll think about your habit throughout the day are increased.
- Environment design is powerful not only because it influences how we engage with the world but also because we rarely do it.
- The objects in the environment do not define our behavior, it's our relationship to them that defines our behavior.
- Stop viewing your environment as though it's filled with objects, think about it as though it's filled with relationships.
- It is easier to link a new habit with a new context, than to develop a new habit in the face of opposing cues.
- When getting an entirely new environment becomes difficult or even impossible, redefine or rearrange your current environment.

Answer the following questions as sincerely as you can:

1. The next time you go shopping, what one thing will happen for you to know that you have begun building good hopping habits? Will you buy every product you're seeing for the first time? Will you reach for products tucked away in harder-to-reach spots? What is it? Pen it down.

_____

_____

_____

_____

_____

_____

2. The less obviously available a product or service is, the less likely you are to try it.

   True [ ] False [ ]

3. Items at eye level tend to be purchased more than those down near the floor. Do you agree with this assertion? **Yes, I do. [ ]   No, I don't. [ ]**

4. List three habits you will initiate by creating obvious visual cues in your environment.

   a. _____

   b. _____

   c. _____

5. State three ways you can redesign your environment and make the cues for your preferred habits more obvious:

   a. _____

   b. _____

   c. _____

6. Think deeply about two consistent habits you currently do. What are their triggers? Write them down.

Habits	**Triggers**
a. _____	_____
b. _____	_____

7. Having identified the triggers to the habits listed in question 7 above, what contextual changes will you make so as to change these habits easier?

_____

_____

_____

_____

_____

_____

8. In what ways are you willing to redefine or rearrange your
   current environment?

_____

_____

_____

_____

_____

_____

Chapter Seven: The Secret to Self-Control

Here are some key points we learned in this chapter:

- Those who have the best self-control usually need to use it the least.

- When you do not have to use self-control often, it becomes easier to practice it.

- You cannot improve your qualities by merely wishing you were more disciplined. The best way to go about improving your qualities is by creating a more disciplined environment for yourself.

- Any habit which has been fixed in the mind is ready to be used whenever the applicable situation arises.

- The moment a habit has been encoded, whenever the environmental cues surface, there is an urge to act.

- If you do not pay careful attention to cues, you may end up creating and causing the very behavior you intend to stop.

- Bad habits strengthen the feelings they attempt to kill.

- It is possible to break a habit. It is however very unlikely that you'll forget it.

- As long as the mental grooves of habits have been etched into your brain, removing them completely might be no less than an impossibility.

- One of the most ineffective strategies that exists is simply resisting temptation. It's a recipe for failure.

- A very practical way to get rid of a bad habit reducing exposure to the cue that causes it.
- Ensure that you make the cues of your good habits noticeable and the cues of your bad habits unseen.

Answer the following questions as sincerely as you can:

1. Within the next couple of days, how do you intend to spend less time in tempting situations? Will you wish you were a more disciplined person everyday? Will you create a more disciplined environment? What practical steps will you employ? State them here.

   _____

   _____

   _____

   _____

   _____

   _____

2. Discipline would solve all our problems. **True [ ]   False [ ]**

3. Behavior change techniques can backfire. **True [ ]   False [ ]**

4. Pause for a moment and reflect on your life. Have there been situations where the cues you used, or the cues you were shown led you right back to the behavior you were trying to stop? List those situations.

   a. _____

   b. _____

c. _____

d. _____

5. Have you ever tried the temptation resistance strategy? How successful was it? Describe your experience.

_____

_____

_____

_____

6. State five bad habits you have. Identify the sources of these habits as well.

Habits	**Sources**
a. _____	_____
b. _____	_____
c. _____	_____
d. _____	_____
e. _____	_____

7. One of the most practical ways to eliminate a bad habit is to reduce exposure to the cue that causes it. In practical terms, how do you intend to apply this strategy to the habits listed above?

_____

_____

_____

_____

_____

_____

_____

8. What good habits do you currently practice? List them below.

    a. _____

    b. _____

    c. _____

    d. _____

Chapter Eight: How to Make a Habit Irresistible

Here are some key points we learned in this chapter:

- As humans, it is very natural to fall for inflated versions of reality.

- The greater the attraction an opportunity possesses, the greater the chances of it becoming habit-forming.

- The world we live in today is filled with extremely concocted versions of reality which are way more attractive than the world our ancestors grew in.

- The trend is that stimuli becomes more enticing, while rewards become more concentrated.

- To increase the odds that a behavior will occur, you must make it attractive.

- Habits are a dopamine-driven feedback loop. Any behavior which is highly habit-forming is linked to higher levels of dopamine. This can also be said for our rather basic, typical behaviors like having sex, eating and interacting socially.

- Dopamine is released on two occasions- when you experience pleasure, and when you anticipate it.

- The human brain has way more neural circuitry dedicated to wanting rewards than to liking rewards.

- The engine that propels behavior is known as desire. Every action is taken as a result of the eagerness that heralds it. This craving is what leads to the response.

- There is a major reason for which we have to make our habits attractive- the expectation of a rewarding experience motivates us to act in the very first place.

- One way to make your habits more attractive is through temptation bundling. This strategy employs pairing an action you want to do with an action you need to do.

- There is a greater chance that you'll find a behavior attractive if you get to do it alongside one of your favorite things.

Answer the following questions as sincerely as you can:

1. You are aware that placing a high value on salt, sugar, and fat are of no benefits to your health, yet the cravings for these food items remain. Having been armed with this information, what will you do differently? What practical steps will you employ? State them here.

_____

_____

_____

_____

_____

_____

2. The higher the attraction an opportunity carries, the more likely it is to become habit-forming. **True [ ] False [ ]**

3. Dopamine is released only when you experience pleasure. **True [ ] False [ ]**

4. Which of the following get us to take action? **The anticipation of a reward [ ]   The fulfillment of a reward [ ]**

5. To increase the odds that a behavior will occur, you need to make it:
   a. **Biological**
   b. **Attractive**
   c. **Concentrated**

6. State five things/ habits you need to do.
   a. _____
   b. _____
   c. _____
   d. _____
   e. _____

7. To increase your chances of carrying out the five habits listed above, apply temptation bundling to each habit in order to make it more attractive.
   a. _____
   b. _____
   c. _____
   d. _____
   e. _____

8. In line with habit stacking, create a set of rules to guide your behavior.
   a. _____

b. _____

c. _____

d. _____

e. _____

Chapter Nine: The role of Family and Friends in Shaping Your Habits

Here are some key points we learned in this chapter:

- One of the deepest human desires is to belong.

- Our earliest habits aren't chosen by us. They come by way of imitation from friends, family, church, school, local communities and the society at large.

- More often than not, we blindly follow our culture's habits- without reasoning, without enquiring, and sometimes, without recalling.

- When behaviors help us fit in, they are attractive.

- There are three groups whose habits we imitate- the close, the many and the powerful.

- We pick up habits from those around us.

- As a general rule, the closer we are to someone, the more likely we are to imitate some of their habits.

- We absorb the qualities and values of those around us.

- An effective means to building better habits is to become part of a culture where the behavior you desire is normal.

- In cases where we are unsure of how we act; we turn to the group to guide our behavior.

- The behavior which the tribe considers normal often overshadows the individual's desired behavior.

- Being accepted is a big deal. The reward that comes with being accepted is often greater than the rewards gotten from winning arguments, appearing smart or even finding the truth.

- If changing your habits would mean challenging the tribe, then, change becomes unattractive. However, when changing your habits means that you fit in with the tribe, change becomes very attractive.
- The major reason why we try to copy the behavior of successful people is because we also desire success. The bulk of our daily habits are imitations of persons whom we admire.
- Persons in high-status enjoy the approval, respect, and praise of others. This therefore means that if a behavior can get us approval, respect, and praise, we find it attractive.

Answer the following questions as sincerely as you can:

1. We often imitate the behaviors of people around us without even realizing it. Bearing this in mind, what will you do to build better habits for yourself? Will you read a book? Will you to join a culture where your desired behavior is the normal behavior? Regardless of what the action steps you intend on carrying out are, pen them down.

_____

_____

_____

_____

_____

_____

2. How many groups habits do we imitate, as humans? **One [ ]**
   Two [ ] Three [ ]

3. Everyone wants to belong. **True [ ] False [ ]**

4. Pause for a minute, and think about five habits you picked up
   from the people around you without realizing- parents, friends,
   siblings, e.t.c. Now, write them down below.

   a. _____

   b. _____

   c. _____

   d. _____

   e. _____

5. State one new habit you intend to build.

   _____

   _____

   _____

6. Identify a culture with whom you have something in common,
   and where your desired behavior is the normal behavior. What
   culture will that be?

   _____

   _____

   _____

7. Having understood that challenging the tribe makes your
   change unattractive, would you rather be wrong with the
   crowd than be right by yourself? **Yes [ ] No [ ]**

8. Provide reason(s) for your choice in Question 7 above.

_____

_____

_____

_____

_____

_____

9. Look inwards. In what ways have you been trying to stand out?

_____

_____

_____

_____

_____

_____

10. What behaviors have you unconsciously avoided in order not to lower your status?

_____

_____

_____

_____

_____

_____

Chapter Ten: How to Find and Fix the Causes of Your Bad Habits

Here are some key points we learned in this chapter:

- Every behavior that you see has a deeper, fundamental motive.

- Your habits are a combination of contemporary solutions to olden desires. In other words, they are simply new versions of already existing vices.

- In all honesty, your present habits are not actually the best way to solve the problems you might be contending with. Rather, they are simply the methods you learned to use.

- The minute you are able to associate a solution with the problem you have to solve, you will keep coming back to it.

- Habits are essentially about associations. These associations are powerful enough to determine whether or not we envisage a habit to be worth repeating.

- Our behavior relies heavily on how we interpret the events that happen to us, and not necessarily the non-subjective reality of the events themselves.

- Your habits are actually caused by the prediction that precedes them. This prediction is what leads to a feeling.

- The difference between where you presently are and where you want to be in the future is desire.

- When we associate habits with positive feelings, they are attractive. We can use this revelation positively, rather than to a disadvantage.

- When you associate bad habits with positive experiences, you make them more attractive.
- You can find and fix the causes of your bad habits by reframing the associations you currently hold about them.
- By reprogramming your predictions, you can convert a difficult habit into an attractive one.
- To create a motivation ritual, simply do something you enjoy right before a difficult habit.

Answer the following questions as sincerely as you can:

1. Over the next one year, what will happen to help you determine whether you've been able to train your brain to enjoy bad habits, or not? Is it your approach to such habits? Is it a mid-set shift? Is it a change in the words you use? Pen it down.

_____

_____

_____

_____

_____

_____

2. Reframing the associations you have about your bad habits is the most effective way to find and fix their causes. **True [ ] False [ ]**

3. List some of your underlying motives for any of your behaviors

_____

_____

_____

4. How do you address these underlying motives?

_____

_____

_____

_____

_____

_____

_____

_____

5. In this moment, what do you notice about yourself?

_____

_____

_____

_____

_____

6. Take a five-minute break before returning to this workbook. Walk around. Return to your previous position. Has anything changed? What action did you take in response to the change?

_____

_____

_____

_____

_____

_____

7. At present, what is your greatest habit desire?

_____

_____

_____

_____

_____

_____

8. List five habits that have been otherwise hard for you to build

_____

_____

_____

_____

_____

_____

_____

_____

9. Now, associate these hard habits with positive experiences by simply changing one word from each sentence stated above. E.g.; *You don't "have" to study, you "get" to study.*

_____

_____

_____

_____

_____

_____

_____

_____

10. In one sentence each, reframe five habits to highlight their benefits rather than their drawbacks.

a. _____

_____

_____

b. _____

_____

_____

c. _____

_____

_____

d. _____

_____

_____

e. _____

_____

_____

Chapter Eleven: Walk Slowly, but Never Backward

Here are some key points we learned in this chapter:

- In a bid to find the optimal plan for change, it is quite easy to get bogged down.

- While in motion, you're doing a lot of learning, planning and strategizing. However, as good as all these are, they do not produce results. On the flip side, the type of behavior that will deliver an outcome is action.

- Motion is a phenomenon which permits us to feel as though we are actually making progress in our lives without attaching the risk of failure.

- It's easy to be in motion and convince yourself that you're still making progress.

- The key to master a habit is beginning with repetition rather than perfection. You do not need to figure out every feature of a new habit. All you need to do is to practice it.

- The process through which a behavior becomes gradually more automatic through repetition is known as habit formation. By repeating an activity more and more, the structure of your brain changes to become efficient at that activity.

- Physical and clear changes in the brain are attained when a habit is repeated.

- All habits go through a similar route beginning with effortful practice to automatic behavior. This process is known as automaticity. Automaticity refers to the ability to perform a behavior without consciously thinking about each step. Automaticity occurs when the nonconscious mind takes control.

- In the real sense of things, the length of time it takes for a habit to become automatic does not really matter. What matters most is that you take all the necessary actions needed to make progress. It is of less importance bothering about whether or not an action is fully automatic.

- In order to build a habit, you must practice it. The most efficient way of making sure that practice happens is by adhering to the 3rd Law of Behavior Change: Make it easy.

Answer the following questions as sincerely as you can:

1. How will you discover or measure your growth with regards to taking action? By realizing that your planning game has become stronger? When you notice that drafting strategies have become easy to do? When you make a move actually to carry out that habit? What is it? State it below.

_____

_____

_____

_____

_____

_____

2. Motion leads to results. **True [ ]   False [ ]**

3. Which of these don't you do while in motion?

Plan [ ]

Strategize [ ]

Take action [ ]

 Learn [ ]

4. Reflect on your life. In what ways have you continually been in motion, but have constantly refused to take action? State them here.

_____

_____

_____

_____

_____

_____

5. Having identified your 'motions' in Question 4 above, what are the necessary action steps to take in order to produce results?

_____

_____

_____

_____

_____

_____

6. The more you repeat an activity, the more your brain's structure changes to become efficient at that activity. Think about three skills you're good at as results of repetitively

having to learn them. E,g, Playing the guitar. List these skills below

_____

_____

_____

7. Over the next two weeks, what lifestyle habits are you willing to repeat in order to establish habits?

_____

_____

_____

_____

_____

_____

8. Are you willing to take the actions you need to take to make progress? **Yes [ ]   No [ ]**

Chapter Twelve: The Law of Least Effort

Here are some key points we learned in this chapter:

- The wisdom that goes around holds that the key to habit change is motivation. However, the real motivation is being lazy and doing the things that are convenient for us.

- Energy is a precious gift, and the brain is wired in such a way that it conserves it whenever possible.

- Following the Law of Least Effort is a human nature. This law basically states that on a natural level, people will tilt towards the option which requires the least amount of work when deciding between two similar options.

- We are motivated to do what is easy.

- Every action needs a certain amount of energy. The more the energy required to carry out the action, the lower the chances of its occurrence.

- Take a look at any behavior occupying a huge percentage of your life, you'll realize that it can be performed with very low levels of motivation.

- You are skilled to do very difficult things. The problem is that while you feel like doing the hard work on certain days, it might not be the same on other days. On the days when it is tough, it is important that you have several things working in your favor so that you can overcome the challenges that life deals you with.

- If you face less friction, your stronger self finds it easier to emerge.

- The idea behind make it easy goes beyond doing easy things. The idea is to make it as easy as possible in the moment to do things that payoff in the long run.
- One of the most effective ways by which you can reduce the friction associated with your habits is to practice environment design.
- It is easier to build habits when they fit into the flow of your life.
- Most of the battle of building better habits boils down to discovering ways to reduce the friction linked with our good habits and increase the friction connected to our bad ones.

Answer the following questions as sincerely as you can:

1. Priming your environment for immediate use can happen in several ways. For persons interested in cooking healthy breakfasts, they may decide to place the skillet on the stove, set the cooking spray on the counter, and lay out any plates and utensils they'll need the night before. Upon waking, making breakfast becomes a seamless task. What will your prime your environment for? How do you intend to go about it?

_____

_____

_____

_____

_____

2. Africa and the Americas have North-South as their axis. **True [ ] False [ ]**

3. What are our real motivations?

    a. **Laziness and Convenience [ ]**

    b. **Desire and Action [ ]**

    c. **Wisdom and Strategy [ ]**

4. The less energy a habit requires, the more likely it is to occur. List three cases in your life where this statement has proved to be true.

    a. _____

    b. _____

    c. _____

5. List three habits, stating how they are obstacles to getting what you really want. E.g.; *Dieting is an obstacle to getting fit.*

    a. _____

    b. _____

    c. _____

6. List three habits, explaining how to make them convenient to enable you follow through with them.

    a. _____

    b. _____

    c. _____

7. In what ways can you optimize your environment to make actions easier?

a. _____

b. _____

c. _____

8. Enumerate the points of friction that have held you back from being effective in your habit building?

    a. _____

    b. _____

    c. _____

    d. _____

Chapter Thirteen: How to Stop Procrastinating by Using the Two-Minute Rule

Here are some key points we learned in this chapter:

- About forty to fifty percent of the actions we perform any given day are borne out of habit.

- Habits are choices, automatic choices which influence the mindful decisions that follow.

- Habits lead you down a path and, jut before you know it, you're speeding on your way to a next behavior.

- It appears easier to continue what you are used to doing rather than start a new habit.

- On a daily basis, there are several moments that deliver an outsized impact. These tiny choices are moments of decisions. These moments set and create the options which will then be available to you in the future.

- Our limitations are founded by where our habits lead us. This explains why it is important that we master the decisive moments throughout your day. Every day is made up of several moments, but the path you take is decided by a few habitual choices.

- The minute you begin doing the right thing, it becomes easier to continue doing it.

- Usually, you can map out the gateway habits which will lead to your desired outcome. This can be achieved by mapping out your goals on a scale from "very easy" to "very hard."

- Before a habit can be improved, it must be established. If you fail to learn the basic skill of showing up, your chances of mastering the finer details are slim.
- The more you ritualize the beginning of a process, the more likely it becomes that you can slip into the state of deep focus that is required to do great things.
- Practically any larger life goal can be transformed into a two-minute behavior.
- If you struggle to stick with a habit, employ the Two-Minute Rule.

Answer the following questions as sincerely as you can:

1. On a daily basis, there are several moments that produce an outsized impact. These little choices, like we know are referred to s decisive moments. How well can you say you have mastered the decisive moments throughout your day?

   _____
   _____
   _____
   _____
   _____
   _____

2. We are limited by where our habits lead us. **True [ ]**
   False [ ]

3. Habits are which of the following?
   a. **The End point [ ]**
   b. **The cab [ ]**

c. The entry point [   ]

d. The gym [   ]

4. What do you understand by the two-minute rule? Is it logical?

_____

_____

_____

_____

_____

_____

5. Scale any three habits down into a two-minute version

a. _____

b. _____

c. _____

6. It is important that you know what your gateway habits are. To figure them out, map your goals on a scale from "very easy" to "very hard." Now, list the goals that fall into the "very easy" category below:

a. _____

b. _____

c. _____

d. _____

7. Using the habit shaping technique, expand your two-minute rule up toward your ultimate goal with just three habits.

a. _____

b. _____

_____

_____

c. _____

_____

_____

8. Does this technique reinforce the identity you want to build?

   Yes [ ]   No [ ]

Chapter Fourteen: How to Make Good Habits Inevitable and Bad Habits Impossible

Here are some key points we learned in this chapter:

- In some cases, success doesn't border on making good habits easy as much as it does about making bad habits hard.

- If you find yourself in a situation where you continually struggle to follow through on your plans, make your bad habits more difficult by simply creating a commitment device.

- A commitment device is a decision you make in the present which controls your actions in the future. The commitment device is a way to lock in future behavior, get you bound to bind good habits as well as restrict you from bad ones.

- The key of the commitment device is changing the task in such a way that it requires more work to get out of the good habit than to get started on it.

- They increase the odds that you'll do right in the future by making bad habits difficult, presently.

- The best way to successfully break a bad habit is by making it impractical to do.

- Technology can convert actions that were once difficult, complex and irritating into behaviors that are easy, painless, and simple.

- When you are able to automate as much of your life as possible, you can expend your effort on the tasks that machines cannot do yet. Each habit that we leave to the authority of technology frees up time and energy to pour into the next stage of our growth.

- When the effort needed to act on your desires becomes effectually zero, you can find yourself sliding into whatever impulse arises at the moment.
- The disadvantage of automation is that we can find ourselves hopping from easy task to easy task without creating time for more difficult, but eventually more worthwhile, work.
- By making use of commitment devices, strategic onetime decisions, and technology, you can create an environment of inescapability—a space where good habits are more than just an outcome which is hoped for, but one that is virtually guaranteed.

Answer the following questions as sincerely as you can:

1. A lot of people find it difficult following through on their plans. A year from today, what would you record as having grown past this difficulty? Will you create devices to keep you committed? Will you do things at your pace, saying you can only do the much that you can? What steps will you take to conclude that this difficulty is past you? State them below.

_____

_____

_____

_____

_____

_____

2. Fill in the blank spaces in this statement. We can make good habits _____ and bad habits _____ .

   a. Inevitable, Impossible [   ]

   b. Manual, Automated [   ]

   c. Impossible, Inevitable [   ]

   d. Automated, Manual [   ]

3. The best way to break a bad habit is to make it impractical to do. **True [   ] False [   ]**

4. List three bad habits you're willing to break

   a. _____

   b. _____

   c._____

5. State three one-time actions that can lock in good habits.

   a._____

   b._____

   c._____

6. Make a list of five one-time actions that lock in good habits across various areas of your life.

   a._____

   b._____

   c._____

   d._____

   e._____

7. Automating your life as much as possible will help free up time and energy.

True [ ] False [ ]

8. State three ways in which you have to be careful, so that the power of technology does not work against you.

    a._____

    b._____

    c._____

Chapter Fifteen: The Cardinal Rule of Behavior Change

Here are some key points we learned in this chapter:

- When our experience is satisfying, we are more likely to repeat a behavior.

- One thing your brain learns from pleasure is that a behavior is worth remembering and repeating.

- Learning what to do in the future is often based on the things you were rewarded for doing, or punished for doing, in the past.

- Positive emotions are responsible for cultivating habits. Negative emotions destroy habits.

- The first three laws of behavior change increase the odds that a behavior will be performed this time.

- The fourth law of behavior change- increases the odds that a behavior will be repeated next time.

- The fourth law of behavior change completes the habit loop.

- In our current society, most of the choices you make today will not benefit you immediately.

- The way your brain assesses rewards is unpredictable across time. You value the present more than you value the future.

- The minute you're able to understand how the brain prioritizes rewards, the answers become clear: the consequences of bad habits are delayed, while the rewards are immediate.

- Every habit births multiple outcomes across time. Sadly, these outcomes are often misaligned.

- With our bad habits, the immediate outcome usually feels good, but the ultimate outcome feels bad. With good habits, the immediate outcome is unenjoyable, but the ultimate outcome feels good.
- Whatever is rewarded immediately is repeated. What is punished immediately is avoided.
- The crucial thing in getting a habit to stick is to feel successful, no matter how tiny this feeling of success is. The feeling of success is an indication that your habit paid off and that the work was worth the sweat.
- The conclusion of any experience is crucial because we tend to remember it more than other phases.

Answer the following questions as sincerely as you can:

1. The lack of satisfaction from an experience may cause us not to repeat such experience. This is what happens with the regular man. Having read and ingested the principles that guide this attitude, what are you willing to do to ensure that your hard habits become satisfying so as to enjoy repetition?

_____

_____

_____

_____

_____

_____

2. Think about three bad habits you currently have. List them below, paired with their immediate satisfactions.

Habit	*Immediate Satisfaction*
a. _____	_____
b. _____	_____
c. _____	_____

3. How do you delay gratification?

   _____

   _____

   _____

   _____

   _____

4. You're trying to build a new habit. To make it stick, you need to feel successful about it. Think about a good habit you're trying to develop. How do you feel successful while at it?

   _____

   _____

   _____

   _____

   _____

   _____

5. If you applied the avoidance technique, how would it help in the development of your desired habit?

   _____

   _____

   _____

   _____

_____

_____

6. List three ways in which you might have been casting votes
   for conflicting identities. E.g., rewarding yourself for exercising
   with a bowl of ice cream.

   a. _____

   b. _____

   c. _____

7. State 3 strategies you can adopt to make your new habit
   enjoyable.

   a. _____

   _____

   _____

   b. _____

   _____

   _____

   c. _____

   _____

   _____

Chapter Sixteen: How to Stick with Good Habits Every Day

Here are some key points we learned in this chapter:

- It is satisfying when you make progress. Visual measures such as moving paper clips or hairpins or marbles all make clear evidence of your progress available.

- A simple way to measure whether a habit was performed or not is to use a habit tracker.

- Habit tracking is powerful. This is because it leverages multiple Laws of Behavior Change. It concurrently makes a behavior noticeable, attractive, and sufficient.

- By merely tracking a behavior, the urge to change it can be sparked.

- Habit tracking keeps you honest. Measurement offers one way to overcome our blindness to our own behavior and notice what's really going on each day.

- The most effective form of motivation is progress. When we get a signal that we are moving forward, we become more motivated to continue down that path.

- Tracking can become its own form of reward.

- Habit tracking helps keep your eye on the ball. You place more attention on the process rather than the result.

- Tracking isn't for everyone. Also, there isn't any need to measure your entire life.

- Whenever possible, measurement should be automated.

- Limit manual tracking to your most important habits. It is better to constantly and devotedly track one habit than to infrequently track ten.

- Make sure you record each measurement right after the habit occurs. Completing the behavior is the prompt to write it down.

- Regardless of how consistent you are with your habits; it is unavoidable that life will interrupt you at some point. There is no perfection anywhere. Whenever this comes into play, remember this: never miss twice.

- When you miss once, it is considered an accident. However, missing twice heralds a new habit.

- The ugly side to tracking a particular behavior is that we become motivated by the number rather than the purpose behind it.

- Measurement is only beneficial when it directs you and adds context to a larger picture. Measurement is of no benefit when it consumes you. Each number is just one piece of reaction in the overall system.

Answer the following questions as sincerely as you can:

1. It's one thing to make progress; it's another to know you're making progress. Knowing this can only come by way of measurement. Going forward, how do you plan on measuring progress in your habits? Will you use the paper clip strategy? Will you make use of marbles? Whatever you decide to do, state it below.

_____

_____

_____

_____

_____

_____

2. Have you ever tried to measure your progress at keeping up with a habit before?

   Yes [ ]   No [ ]

3. If your response to Question 3 above was 'yes', how did you go about it? Was it effective?

   _____

   _____

   _____

   _____

   _____

   _____

4. If your response to Question 3 above was 'no', why haven't you tried it? What are your concerns?

   _____

   _____

   _____

   _____

   _____

   _____

5. A habit tracker is vital. What kind of tracker will be effective in the building of your desired habit?

_____

_____

_____

6. How effective will your chosen habit tracker be to the actualization of your desired habit? Why do you think so?

_____

_____

_____

_____

_____

_____

7. Using your current and desired habits, create three different examples of habit stacking + habit tracking formula. E.g.; *After I hang up the phone from a sales call, I will move one paper clip over.*

a. _____

_____

_____

b. _____

_____

_____

c. _____

_____

_____

Chapter Seventeen: How an Accountability Partner Can Change Everything

Here are some key points we learned in this chapter:

- In the same way we most likely will repeat an experience when the ending is satisfying, we will also most likely avoid an experience when the ending is painful.

- When a failure is painful, it gets fixed. However, when a failure is painless, it gets ignored.

- The more immediate and more costly a mistake is, the faster you will learn from it.

- To prevent bad habits and eliminate unhealthy behaviors, add an instant cost to the action.

- The main reason why we repeat bad habits is because they serve us in some way. This is why it also becomes difficult to abandon them.

- As soon as actions incur an immediate consequence, behavior begins to change.

- There is a shift in behavior only if the punishment is painful enough and steadfastly enforced.

- The more immediate, concrete, local and tangible the consequence is, the higher the likelihood that it will influence individual behavior. However, the more global, intangible, vague, and delayed the consequence, the less likely it is to influence individual behavior.

- To make bad habits unsatisfying, the best bet is to make them painful in the moment. Creating a habit contract is an upfront way to get that done.
- Being aware that you're being watched by someone else can be a powerful motivator.
- The presence of an accountability partner can create an immediate cost to inaction. Because we care deeply about what others think of us, we do not want them to have a lesser opinion of us.

Answer the following questions as sincerely as you can:

1. Understanding that by making your failures result in pain, you are more likely to avoid such; what measures are you willing to put in place to ensure that you do not repeat unhealthy behaviors that can result in pain?

   _____

   _____

   _____

   _____

   _____

   _____

2. We repeat bad habits because they serve us in some way. True [   ]   False [   ]

3. The more _____ a consequence, the more likely it is to influence individual behavior.
   a. **Local [   ]**

b. Delayed [   ]

c. Global [   ]

4. What is your ideal outcome for the habit you're currently trying to build?

    _____

    _____

5. Create a three-phased roadmap to achieve your ideal outcome.

    Phase 1

    _____

    _____

    _____

    _____

    _____

    Phase 2

    _____

    _____

    _____

    _____

    _____

    Phase 3

    _____

    _____

    _____

_____

_____

6. Write down the daily habits that would lead you to your goal
   (assuming this is a 1-month goal)

   1. _____
   2. _____
   3. _____
   4. _____
   5. _____
   6. _____
   7. _____
   8. _____
   9. _____
   10. _____
   11. _____
   12. _____
   13. _____
   14. _____
   15. _____
   16. _____
   17. _____
   18. _____
   19. _____
   20. _____
   21. _____
   22. _____
   23. _____
   24. _____
   25. _____

26._____

27._____

28._____

29._____

30._____

31._____

7. Design punishments you would have to experience if you fail to follow through your roadmap at each phase.

Phase 1 punishment

_____

_____

_____

_____

_____

Phase 2 punishment

_____

_____

_____

_____

_____

Phase 3 punishment

_____

_____

_____

_____

Chapter Eighteen: The Truth About Talent (When Genes Matter and When They Don't)

Here are some key points we learned in this chapter:

- The secret to making the most of your odds of success is choosing the right field of competition.

- It is easier to perform and stick with habits when they align with your natural predispositions and abilities.

- The strength of genetics is also their weakness. Genes cannot be easily changed. This means they provide a prevailing lead in favorable circumstances and a grave hindrance in unfavorable circumstances.

- Our environment determines the appropriateness of our genes and the usefulness of our natural talents. When our environment changes, the qualities that determine success change as well.

- Those at the top of any competitive field are well trained and well suited to the task. In order to be truly great, it is important that you select the right place to focus.

- Your destiny is not determined by your genes. Your genes determine your areas of opportunity.

- Beneath the surface of every habit, your genes are operational.

- Your personality is the set of characteristics that is consistent from situation to situation.

- Our habits are not solely determined by our personalities. Our deeply rooted preferences make certain behaviors easier for some people than for others.
- You don't have to build the habits everyone tells you to build. Choose habits that best suit you, not habits that are most popular.
- In order to maintain motivation and feel successful, it is important that you learn to play a game where the odds are in your favor.
- Those talented in a particular area tend to be more skilled at that task.
- If you pick the right habit, progress becomes easy. If you pick the wrong habit, life becomes a struggle.
- The goal is to try out many options, research a broad range of ideas, and cast a wide net.

Answer the following questions as sincerely as you can:

1. What habits are you naturally inclined towards? Write them down.

    a. _____

    b. _____

    c. _____

2. If you had to choose your 'right field of competition' to develop a habit around, what would this be?

    _____

3. Do you accept that people are born with different abilities? **Yes [ ] No [ ]**

4. Give reasons for your choice in Question 3 above. Provide instances or scientific evidence to back up your reason.

_____

_____

_____

_____

_____

_____

5. Based on the five spectrums of behavior explored in this book, which of these would you say is your personality type?
   a. **Openness to experience [ ]**
   b. **Conscientiousness [ ]**
   c. **Extroversion [ ]**
   d. **Agreeableness [ ]**
   e. **Neuroticism [ ]**

6. Why do you think you belong to the spectrum of behavior chosen in Question 5 above? Provide justifications for your choice.

_____

_____

_____

_____

_____

7. In your opinion, what three habits best suit your personality?

a. _____

b. _____

c. _____

8. It is evident that picking the wrong habit may be difficult to go through with. How then do you pick the right habit? Trial and error? Spending more time on the habit of your dreams regardless of whether it's wrong, or right? Whatever method you believe will help you pick the right habit, write it down.

_____

_____

_____

_____

_____

_____

Chapter 19: The Goldilocks Rule: How to Stay Motivated in Life and Work

Here are a few key points we learned from this chapter:

- The human brain loves a challenge as long as it lies within an optimum zone of difficulty.

- The Goldilocks Rule posits that humans experience highest motivation when working on tasks that are right on the edge of their current abilities. Not too hard. Not too easy. Just right.

- When starting a new habit, it's important that you keep the behavior as easy as possible so that you can stick with it even when conditions aren't perfect.

- The minute a habit has been established; it becomes important to gradually advance in small ways. These little enhancements and new tests keep you engaged.

- If you hit the Goldilocks Zone perfectly, you can achieve a flow state.

- A flow state is the experience of being in the zone and being fully absorbed in an activity.

- To achieve a state of flow, a task must be roughly 4 per cent above your current ability.

- You have to constantly search for challenges that push you to your edge while proceeding to make enough progress to stay motivated.

- Behaviors need to remain innovative in order for them to stay striking and sustaining.

- Mastery entails practice. However, the more you devote time to practicing something, it becomes more routine and boring.
- The greatest threat to success is boredom. We get bored with habits because we stop taking pleasure in them.
- As our habits start to get ordinary, we start derailing our progress to seek innovation.
- The instant we experience the least dip in enthusiasm, we begin to seek a new strategy, even if the old one was still working.
- If you succeed at starting a habit and are able to keep sticking to it, there will be days when you feel like giving up.
- The difference between a professional and an amateur is stepping up when it's annoying or painful or draining to do so.

Answer the following questions as sincerely as you can:

1. You're trying to build a habit, or habits. It is very possible that rather than pull you in, this habit might fade away. How will you ensure that the habit you're trying to develop pulls you in? Write it down.

   _____
   _____
   _____
   _____
   _____
   _____

2. Have you ever tried challenging your brain within a high difficulty zone? **Yes [ ] No [ ]**

3. What new habit do you desire to establish?

_____

4. State 3 ways in which you can gradually advance this habit upon establishing it?

a. _____

_____

_____

b. _____

_____

_____

c. _____

_____

_____

5. What does a 'flow state' mean to you?

_____

_____

_____

_____

_____

6. Are you willing to continually search for challenges that push you to your edge? **Yes [   ] No [   ]**

7. Provide reasons for your choice in question 6 above.

_____

_____

_____

_____

_____

_____

8. Having understood the demands of your desired habit, state three strategies with which you intend to stay focused when you get bored working on your goals.

   a. _____

   _____

   _____

   _____

   _____

   b. _____

   _____

   _____

   _____

   c. _____

   _____

   _____

   _____

Chapter Twenty: The Downside of Creating Good Habits

Here are some key points we learned from this chapter:

- Every chunk of information which is learned frees up the mental space for more effortful thinking.

- The benefits of habits are not free; they come at a cost.

- The advantage of habits is that we can do things without thinking. The disadvantage of habits is that you get used to doing things a certain way and fail to pay attention to little errors.

- Once a skill has been grasped, there is usually a trivial deterioration in performance over time.

- When you want to make the most of your potential and achieve top levels of performance, you need a more nuanced style.

- Habits are essential, but not enough for mastery. What you actually need is a blend of automatic habits and intentional practice.

- After one habit has been grasped, you have to go back to the exerting part of the work and begin to build the next habit.

- Mastery is the course of thinning your focus to a tiny part of success, reiterating it until you have adopted the skill, and then using this new habit as the underpinning to advance to the next stage of your growth.

Answer the following questions as sincerely as you can:

1. What costs are you willing to pay to enjoy the benefits of habits?

   _____

   _____

   _____

   _____

   _____

2. What habit have you mastered successfully? Write it down.

   _____

3. What is next habit you're willing to build following the mastery of the aforementioned habit?

   _____

4. Design a strategy to review your desired habit.

   _____

   _____

   _____

   _____

   _____

   _____

   _____

5. Why do you suppose that the review strategy stated above will be sufficient for the habit you have chosen? Provide justifications where necessary.

_____

_____

_____

_____

_____

_____

6. Re-define yourself in three steps.

a. _____

_____

_____

b. _____

_____

_____

c. _____

_____

_____

Made in the USA
Monee, IL
07 October 2022